CALYPSO
Cousteau

SIMON & SCHUSTER BOOKS FOR YOUNG READERS
Simon & Schuster Building, Rockefeller Center, 1230 Avenue of
the Americas, New York, New York 10020. Copyright © 1991 by
Hachette, France, and The Cousteau Society, Inc. English translation
copyright © 1992 by The Cousteau Society, Inc. All rights reserved
including the right of reproduction in whole or in part in any form.
Originally published in France by Hachette Jeunesse as *CORAL
VIVANT*. SIMON & SCHUSTER BOOKS FOR YOUNG READERS is a trademark
of Simon & Schuster. Manufactured in Italy. 10 9 8 7 6 5 4 3 2 1

CREDITS
THE COUSTEAU SOCIETY, Captain Jacques-Yves Cousteau,
Jean-Michel Cousteau, Project Director and Editor: Pamela Stacey,
Author: François Sarano, Photo Editor: Judy K. Brody, Research:
Christine Causse, Design Consultant: André Demaison,
Photographers: Richard C. Murphy: cover, 8–10, 14–15, 17, 23–24,
27, 29, François Sarano: 10, 12, 20–21, 22, Chuck Davis: cover, 6–7, 9,
16–17, 28, Didier Noirot: 2–3, 7, 11, back cover, Pamela Stacey: 18–
19, 26, Scott Frier: 19, Roberto Rinaldi: 4–5, back (inset), Veronique
Sarano–Simon: 13, Michel Verdure: 25. Graphic Design: Carmèle
Delivré and François Huertas

Library of Congress Cataloging-in-Publication Data
Corals : the sea's great builders / the Cousteau Society. p. cm.
Summary: Explains how corals grow, what they need to eat, and
how they nourish other animals. 1. Corals—Juvenile literature.
2. Coral reef ecology—Juvenile literature. [1. Corals. 2. Coral reef
ecology. 3. Ecology.] I. Cousteau Society. QL377.C5C68 1992
593.6—dc20 91-34458 CIP ISBN: 0-671-77068-3

The Cousteau Society

CORALS
THE SEA'S GREAT BUILDERS

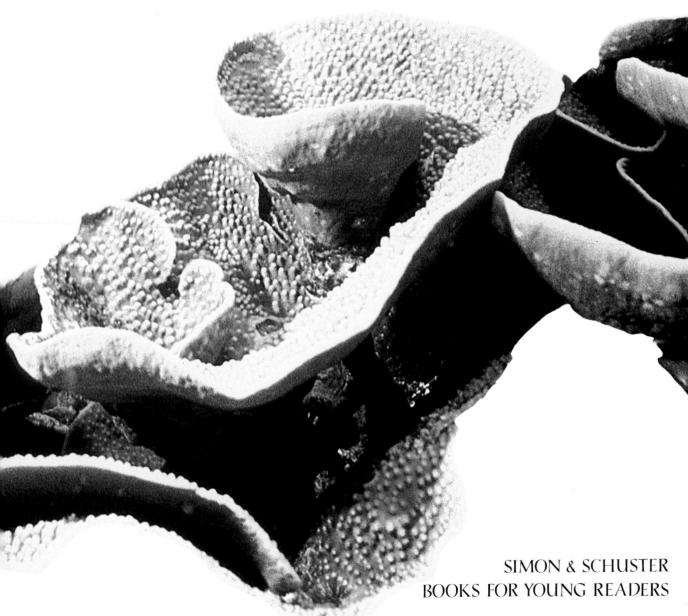

SIMON & SCHUSTER
BOOKS FOR YOUNG READERS

Published by Simon & Schuster
New York London Toronto Sydney Tokyo Singapore

It's a late spring night and the moon is full. Cousteau divers enter warm tropical waters to explore the unusual world of corals in Australia's Great Barrier Reef. They're about to meet an animal that looks like a rock, acts like a plant part of the time, and hunts with a harpoon!

The divers' lights illuminate a garden of stones as soft as velvet. But these stony pillars are alive. Seen up close, they are covered with small, sticky tentacles. Like huge apartment buildings, these structures are home to millions of tiny individual animals: coral polyps.

Looking even closer, the divers observe the polyps. Each polyp's soft mouth closes then opens. Suddenly, out pops a tiny pink ball that rises toward the surface. Then another, and another! All along the reef, coral polyps are releasing tiny balls like miniature balloons, all at the same time. What is this nighttime festival in the sea?

It is an annual event on the reef. The corals release their male and female cells into the sea in an upside-down snowstorm. These cells unite to form an egg. The egg divides itself into two cells, then four, doubling each time. It grows into a larva and settles on the seafloor, where it will turn into an unprotected coral polyp. It will then secrete hard walls and a floor to create its own room.

A coral polyp has a soft, sac-like body with no eyes and no brain. During the day it hides. But at night it comes out from its protective shelter. This polyp is an eager hunter. It captures animals smaller than itself by shooting poisoned, harpoon-like darts from the tentacles that surround its mouth.

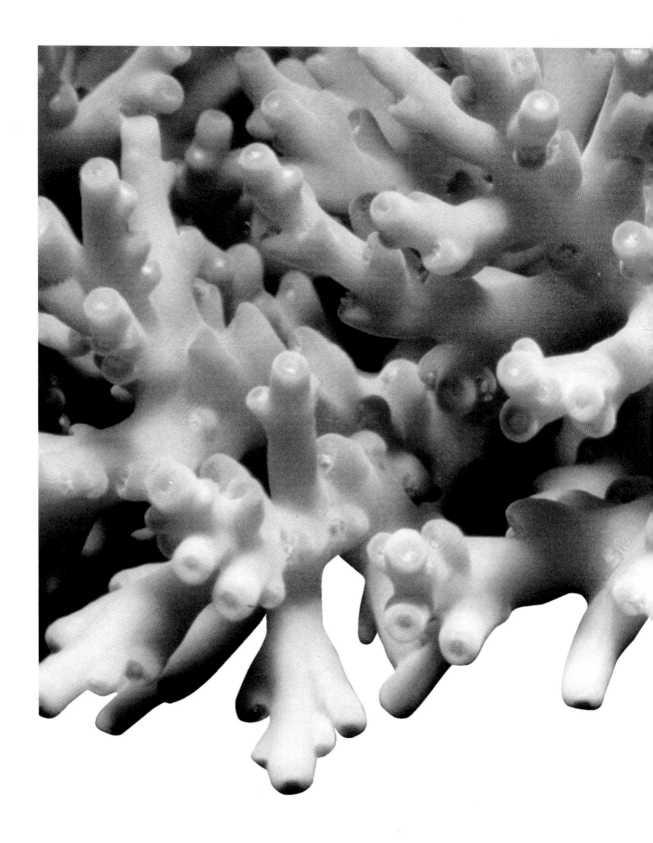

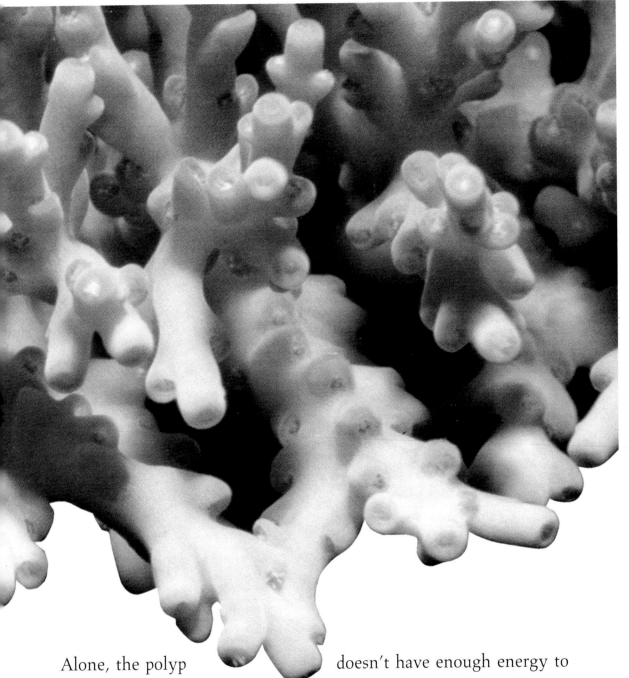

Alone, the polyp doesn't have enough energy to do the work of constructing a huge reef—an entire underwater city—but it has a partner. A very small green sea plant, or alga, lives inside its body. The plant never leaves. The coral protects it and feeds it; in turn, the plant makes food for the coral. Together they form an extraordinary team of builders.

With the plant's help the polyp can build its stone-like room. The polyp then grows by "budding," creating identical polyps. Each polyp then builds its own room. Soon there are hundreds and thousands of polyps. They form a large family, all identical, living in a dwelling they have built. This is a coral colony. It takes millions of coral colonies to create a coral reef.

The colony grows higher and spreads farther and farther across the sea floor. Soon there is no more room to grow. Different colonies struggle and fight for space. They have different kinds of weapons. One uses the poisoned darts of its tentacles. Another shoots out killer threads that quickly digest enemy polyps, leaving only an empty room, and gaining a place on the reef.

Some reef inhabitants find coral good to eat. The crown-of-thorns sea star is the coral's fiercest enemy. Spreading its many arms over the colony, it digests the soft polyps as it crawls. The parrotfish uses its strong beak to crush the hard bits of coral and devour the living polyps.

The lives of many different kinds of fishes depend directly on the living coral reef. The reef also offers hiding places for many small fish. They peek out when there is no danger, but quickly retreat into their hiding places if frightened.

Although they grow only a fraction of an inch each year, coral reefs have become the largest structures created by animals on the planet. Thousands of different animals—like this angelfish or these worms that look like colorful Christmas trees—live inside the reef, protected by the gigantic architecture created over centuries by tiny polyps, the sea's great builders, living corals.